come sweet death

come sweet death

A QUINTET FROM GENESIS

12345

THE GARDEN THE BROTHERS THE FLOOD THE TOWER THE LAND

DAVIE NAPIER

Revised Edition

The Pilgrim Press ● New York

Library of Congress Cataloging in Publication Data

Napier, Bunyan Davie.
  Come sweet death.

  1. Bible. O.T. Genesis—Meditations.
I. Title.
BS1235.4.N3 1981   222'.1106   80-27301
ISBN 0-8298-0422-6 (pbk.)

The scripture quotations at the beginning of each part of the Quintet are
from the *Revised Standard Version of the Bible,* copyrighted 1946 and 1952
by the Division of Christian Education, National Council of Churches, and
are used by permission. The scripture quotations within the remainder of
the text have been adapted by the author.

The Pilgrim Press, 132 West 31 Street, New York, NY 10001

The First Edition is dedicated
to Yale Divinity School and
Calhoun College
Yale University 1949-66
with continuing affection

The Revised Edition is dedicated
to
Stanford University
1966-1972

Pacific School of Religion
1972-1978

First Congregational Church
Eugene, Oregon
1979

"Live the questions now."

contents

part 3

THE FLOOD

Verses from Genesis 6—9

part 4

THE TOWER

Verses from Genesis 11

part 5

THE LAND

Verses from Genesis 12 and 15

introduction to the first edition

The late distinguished German novelist Thomas Mann once said of myth, "It is, it always is, however much men try to say, it was." Of the kind of "events" that are described in the myth form, someone else has said, "These things never were, but always are."

While some of the stories in the early chapters of Genesis are no doubt drawn from myths of the ancient Near East, it is clear that the stories have undergone a theological refinement in the mouths and hands of Israel's tellers and recorders. To a considerable extent the stories have already been demythologized. But in this one regard, they retain the myth quality: the stories exist, they are told and retold, recorded and read and reread not for their *wasness* but for their *isness.*

What follows then is an easy—one almost wants to say "natural"—present-tense (and in a totally nontechnical sense of the word) existential interpretation of the four primary stories in Genesis 2–11: the garden (chapters 2–3), the brothers (chapter 4), the flood (chapters 6–9), and the tower (chapter 11). If these things never were, they always are.

The fifth and final member of this Quintet from Genesis is inspired by the narrative of the call of Abraham in chapter 12. It is a story different in character from those preceding, but at the same time it is, theologically speaking, the climax of all that goes before. In Abraham—who, as the one called forth to find "the land," is everyone and anyone who responds—the coming of the sweet and saving death is made possible. And this, too, always *is.*

introduction to the revised edition

Come Sweet Death was first published in 1967. It has been through five printings; it has been repeatedly quoted in articles, sermons, and anthologies; and parts or all of it have been dramatically "produced" in scores of forms and settings, from choral readings to full dramatizations, from church chancels to college and university and seminary chapels.

Except for a few words, indicated by brackets, I have not altered the language of the *Revised Standard Version of the Bible*, which faithfully reproduces the male-dominated terminology of the underlying Hebrew text. I *have* employed the name Yahweh where it underlies the *Revised Standard Version*'s "the Lord." But in the five verse episodes of *Come Sweet Death*, I have tried in this revision to avoid the representation of God as exclusively male, and the human family as "man." Where the term "man" is retained in the text, I mean precisely the male of the species. Historically speaking, from the plunder and decimation of ancient peoples to the Holocaust and the Vietnam war and the contemporary rape and oppression of the poor and weak by the rich and the powerful, the sorry tale of sustained human carnage is overwhelmingly male-wrought. Towers of all descriptions remain predominantly phallic, from Babel to Lower Manhattan.

If otherwise the language of male chauvinism in reference to God or "man" appears in this revision, it is deliberate; that is, it has seemed to me to be demanded by the characterization of the speaker (e.g., in some of the lines of Cain in Part 2, and the Adversary in Part 3).

The title phrase "Come, sweet death" is first formed in these verse-essays as a bitter human protest: If this is what creation is, then

11

you can take it, Yahweh. But as the textual settings move from Garden to Brothers to Flood to Tower to Land, that title phrase becomes a succinct prayer of petition and gratitude for Jesus Christ—Come, Sweet Death!

It hardly needs to be said that in the context of the book of Genesis, and indeed of the Bible, the first four of the five settings provide the universal backdrop of willful human rebellion and protest against God before which the subsequent biblical drama of Word and People and Prophet and Servant and Christ is played out. Garden, Brothers, Flood, and Tower depict the essential, perennial human condition of destructive pride which begins to be biblically answered in the story of the Land—the purpose of God to bless the families of the earth.

The passage of more than a decade since the first published edition of *Come Sweet Death* leaves me with memories of gratitude for people of all ages who have in so many varied ways confirmed the dictum that if these things never literally were, they always are.

Davie Napier
New Haven, Connecticut

part 12345

THE GARDEN

from Genesis 2—3

7   Then Yahweh God formed man of dust from the ground, and breathed
    into his nostrils the breath of life; and man became a living being.
8   And Yahweh God planted a garden in Eden, in the east; and there he
9   put the man whom he had formed. And out of the ground Yahweh
    God made to grow every tree that is pleasant to the sight and good for
    food, the tree of life also in the midst of the garden, and the tree of the
    knowledge of good and evil.

15   Yahweh God took the man and put him in the garden of Eden to till it
16   and keep it. And Yahweh God commanded the man, saying, "You
17   may freely eat of every tree of the garden; but of the tree of the
     knowledge of good and evil you shall not eat, for in the day that you
     eat of it you shall die."

20   The man gave names to all cattle, and to the birds of the air, and to
     every beast of the field; but for the man there was not found a helper
     fit for him.

22   Yahweh God . . . made . . . a woman and brought her to the
25   man. . . . And the man and his wife were both naked, and were not
     ashamed.

3:1   The serpent . . . said to the woman, "Did God say, 'You shall not eat
 2   of any tree of the garden'?" And the woman said to the serpent, "We
 3   may eat of the fruit of the trees of the garden; but God said, 'You shall
      not eat of the fruit of the tree which is in the midst of the garden,
 4   neither shall you touch it, lest you die.' " But the serpent said to the
 5   woman, "You will not die. For God knows that when you eat of it
      your eyes will be opened, and you will be like God, knowing good
 6   and evil." So when the woman saw that the tree was good for food,
      and that it was a delight to the eyes, and that the tree was to be desired

to make one wise, she took of its fruit and ate; and she also gave some
7   to her husband, and he ate. Then the eyes of both were opened, and
8   they knew that they were naked. . . . And they heard the sound of
Yahweh God walking in the garden in the cool of the day and the man
and his wife hid themselves from the presence of Yahweh God among
9   the trees of the garden. But Yahweh God called to the man, and said
10   to him, "Where are you?" And he said, "I heard the sound of thee in
the garden, and I was afraid, because I was naked; and I hid myself."
11   He said, "Who told you that you were naked? Have you eaten of the
12   tree which I commanded you not to eat?" The man said, "The woman
whom thou gavest to be with me, she gave me fruit of the tree, and I
13   ate." Then Yahweh God said to the woman, "What is this that you
have done?" The woman said, "The serpent beguiled me, and I ate."

16   Yahweh God said . . . to the woman . . . "I will greatly multiply
17   your pain in childbearing. . . ." And to Adam he said, ". . . cursed
19   is the ground because of you; in toil you shall eat of it . . . till you
return to the ground, for out of it you were taken; you are dust, and to
dust you shall return."

23   Therefore Yahweh God sent him forth from the garden of Eden. . . .
24   He drove out the man. . . .

Genesis 2:7–8 *And Yahweh Elohim forms us of dust*
and breathes the breath of life into our nostrils;
and we become a living entity.
God plants a garden in the east (it could as
well be west or south or north), and there
in Eden Yahweh Elohim ordains
that we shall be. . . .

I

This is the garden, Yahweh?
This little plot, this planet earth, this globe
assaulting me in arbitrary sequence
with wind and earthquake, fire, and still small voices;
providing me, in weary alternation,
with snow and sun and rain, seedtime and harvest;
inflicting on me now cacophonous din
and now the sound of thin and gentle silence;
confronting me in sick juxtaposition
with appetizing foods and pesticides,
with cooling drink and nuclear pollution?
This is the garden?

the garden

II

Where, Yahweh, am I?
If this is east, then east of what or whom?
I must be east of you, you big Direction.
Or somewhere east of Suez
on the road to Mandalay
on the road to Mount Olympus
on the road to Canterbury
on the road to Jericho
with pilgrim folk
U.S. Marines
Samaritans
with Alexander
Lewis and Clark
or Don Quixote. . . .
The road! My God, I have to know the road.
I need to go and come and go again.
Your garden is a prison—or a tomb—
without a road.

III

2:15
You call the garden Eden?

Eden schmeeden
tillit schmillit
keepit schmeepit.
So you can take it, God, and keep it, God.
I did not ask you, great I AM, for Eden;
I never made request for garden space.
This place all too apparently is yours;
and no one wants the owner with the space,
not even if the flat is free.

2:20
Besides,

a something indescribable is missing,
a something sweet and soft and warm responding,
a something yielding, melting, something giving,
a something that is something like a dame.
But there is simply nothing like a dame.

IV

2:16–17 You speak a pious, childish doggerel
that sings like "Mary Had a Little Lamb"
  Freely eat of every tree
  every tree every tree
  freely eat of every tree
   nothing I deny
  but the tree of good and evil
  good and evil good and evil
  but the tree of good and evil
   eat of it and die.
Behold, God's wondrous gift is given—with strings.
All glory be to thee, uncertain Giver,
who wants to have the gift and give it too.
I know about your damned restricted tree:
it symbolizes you and your dominion.
To spare its fruit is to acknowledge you.

Now hear this, God: the Giver with the gift
is strictly for the birds and fish and beasts.
I am a Man, made in the godly image,
made to receive and rule the gift of God.
God is for giving. Give, then, and get out.

Go now, Creator, spin some other worlds.
I cut you off, I sever all your moorings.
Drift, God, irrelevant and impotent,
along uncharted seas of vacuous space.
The earth belongs to me, and all its fullness,
the world and every living creature in it;
2:20   since it was I who named each single item
in this vast, complicated, awesome structure.

Dominion given cannot be reclaimed.
By act of God, this land is "man's" dominion
from this day forth, and evermore forever.

V

2:21–25 Now here is something new under the sun.
This place, this little kingdom of a garden
may after all be tolerably fair.
O what a piece of work is woman Eve!
What hath God wrought!

       What have we wrought together,
Yahweh and I, and I and God together.

What have we wrought *together?* Eve is Eve
because I thirst and hunger: Eve exists
to meet my longing, bring to peace my passion,
and all my restlessness to resolution.

So Eve is mine, flesh of my yearning flesh.
Sweet Eve is mine, mother of all creation.

VI

Eve is a fruit tree, Eve a fecund goddess.
I take from Eve the fruit that is forbidden,
3:6   fruit good for food (and for the inward fire);
delightful to the eyes (with tactile gifts);
desired to make one wise (O wisdom sweet).

You hanger-on to life and earth and time
who will alone be loved, adored, and served,
you circumscribing, circumcising Yahweh—
I eat whatever fruit I please to eat.
Right now and any now I'm taking Eve,
which is to say I take dominion here.

I'm taking Eve. I'm taking Ecstasy.
All glory be to thee, O Ecstasy,
Almighty Eve, O Verbless Conjugation,
O Secret, Sacred Wonder of the Meeting.
Hail, Holy Meeting, Mother of the earth,
and farewell, Yahweh—lots of luck to you.

VII

　　Come, Eve, and lie with me
　　under the greenwood tree.
For we are good together, good and evil,
and we are warm together, smooth and warm,
and we are one together, one and one.
Under the greenwood tree no one can see,
not even God, that sexless deity.
　　So come and lie with me
　　under the greenwood tree,
　　the serpent, I, and thee.
We have this time, this Eve, this ecstasy:
we have this knowledge of our nakedness.
So come, sweet Eve, and come sweet ecstasy.

VIII

3:8
Good God, I think it's Yahweh
out walking in the garden
in the coolness of the day.

And looking for a waltz.
Who wants to waltz with Yahweh
in the coolness of the day?

3:9
Where are you? Can't you see, all-seeing Seer?
I'm picking daisies here with Mother Eve,
daisies of good and evil, smooth and warm,
of one and one . . . she loves me, loves me not.
You have some better word on what to do?

3:11
Who told you you were naked? This is good.
Who told me, God? So tell me when I'm drunk;
or maybe that I ought to see the barber;
but I can manage this one by myself.
Or shall I say in abject piety,
"All humankind is naked in thy sight"?

3:11   *Then have you eaten of the tree? The* tree?
        My God! You plant existence in a forest,
        a veritable jungle where one cannot
        discern one's right hand from one's left, and then
        expect me to distinguish tree from tree!
        I skipped the merit badge for trees. I am
        no forest ranger. Trees. Be more specific:
2:9, 17   the tree of life . . . the tree of moral knowledge
        (or is it existential "good and evil"?) . . .
2:9, 3:3 the tree which grows (in Brooklyn) "in the midst"
        (in Birmingham and Belsen "in the midst"
        in Brisbane, Buenos Aires, and the Bronx
        and "in the midst" of Bergen and Beirut,
        of Bombay, Babylon, and Bethlehem—
        that pregnant tree is always in the midst!)
        and finally, compounding this confusion,
        you say without a clarifying word,
3:11   "the tree from which I told you not to eat."

25

Come now, Yahweh, this is ridiculous.
You ask about a tree; almighty God,
forget your silly tree. I will "confess"—
3:12 the woman whom *you* gave to be with me,
she gave me fruit.

3:13   *What have you done?* All right.
No more than this: We take the gift with thanks
but spurn the Giver's counsel for its use;
or at the very worst, the gift accepted,
we ostracize the still-possessive Giver.

3:13 It may be said we were beguiled (a term
in any case untrue, since, if deceived,
we wished to be deceived). But we were not.
We gained the promised knowledge, and we live,
enjoying it.

You are the problem, God.
You *force* us into disobedience—
if disobedience it really is,
and that's a matter simply of perspective.
The theologians want to call it pride
or even by the stronger term, rebellion.
The pious make the charge apostasy
and hypocrites will cry idolatry.
But this is nonsense, God. It is our nature
(you ought to know, who mixed the hot ingredients)
to spurn the docile role of subjugation;
to be not merely creature but creator;
to stand alone; to cherish in ourselves
all requisite resources for renewal;

Isaiah 40:31   to mount with wings as eagles
to run and not be weary
to walk and not to faint.

You give us all creation, to be sure—
then shake a disembodied godly finger
in our face about a special tree.
Well, God Almighty, if you are almighty
let us be free of you—or let us die!

It is the same, you say, you stubborn God?
Then count me out, I say—and come sweet death!

27

IX

Genesis 3:16 *And I will greatly multiply your pain*
3:17   *in bearing children. . . . Cursed is the ground*
    because of you; now eat of it in toil.
3:19   *Since dust you are, to dust you shall return.*
3:23–24   *Then Yahweh Elohim sent them away . . .*
    to till the ground from which they had been taken.

This is a fine romance. A fine romance
this is. A beautiful relationship—
the Potter and the animated clay;
Creator and the free, creative creature;
the Parent and the independent child—
a beautiful relationship is fractured
for nothing but a silly little tree.

For you, an empty, loveless, lonely garden;
for us, a life of meanness and frustration.
Congratulations, God. Good show. Well done.

X

Hosea 11:8

Sweet Eve, you say you thought you heard God laugh?
I heard God say, *"How can I give you up?*
How can I hand you over?" Then a word
about another silly little tree—
an antidotal tree, redemptive tree.
And then—this must be when you thought God laughed—
I think I heard a sob.

I think God wept.

part 12345

THE BROTHERS

from Genesis 4

1 Now Adam knew Eve his wife, and she conceived and bore Cain. . . .

2 And again, she bore his brother Abel. Now Abel was a keeper of sheep, and Cain a tiller of the ground.

4–5 And Yahweh had regard for Abel and his offering, but [none] for Cain and his offering. So Cain was very angry, and his countenance fell.

6 Yahweh said to Cain, "Why are you angry, and why has your

7 countenance fallen? If you do well, will you not be accepted?"

8 Cain said to Abel his brother, "Let us go out to the field." And when they were in the field, Cain rose up against his brother Abel, and

9 killed him. Then Yahweh said to Cain, "Where is Abel your brother?" He said, "I do not know; am I my brother's keeper?"

10 And Yahweh said, "What have you done? The voice of your brother's

11 blood is crying to me from the ground. And now you are cursed from

12 the ground . . . it shall no longer yield to you its strength; you shall be a fugitive and a wanderer on the earth."

13–14 Cain said . . . "My punishment is greater than I can bear. Behold, thou hast driven me this day away from the ground; and from thy face I shall be hidden; . . . and whoever finds me will slay me."

15 And Yahweh put a mark on Cain, lest any who came upon him should kill him.

Now Adam knew his wife, and she conceived
and bore him Cain . . . again: his brother Abel.

I

One was a shepherd, one would till the ground;
one occupied the high land, one the low;
one practiced circumcision, one abhorred it;
one was contemplative, the other bold.
The one was one, the other was the other.

the brothers

One was dark and one was light
one was brown and one was white
one was west and one was east
one was layman one was priest
one was soldier one was sailor
one a blacksmith one a tailor
one was dreamer one a doer
one a caveman one a wooer.

One was one and one the other
each to each a bloody brother
one liked desert one liked rain—
one *is* Abel . . . one *is* Cain.

II

4:3–5 There's Abel over there, the fair-haired Abel,
the tight and tidy Abel—able Abel:
the ordered life, a time for everything;
existence neatly harnessed, firmly reined.

There's Abel over there, the backward Abel.
He stinks, you know, he literally stinks:
   sweats too much and bathes too little,
   fouls his streets with dung and spittle,
the great unwashed. And arrogant! He thinks
that he is God's and all the world is his.

There's Abel over there, the oddball Abel,
Abel who differs—that's all right. But, oh,
how much he cherishes the difference,
not only in himself but in his God!
This Abel has devised an oddball God.
Of course I cannot altogether blame him:
no proper God—the Only God, that is—
would enter into league with such a man.
And what a spectacle my brother makes,
the brazen nonconformist, hatching plots
I know to seize the fruits of all creation.

I hate his guts, I hate the guts of Abel.
I'm sick of Abel, sick to death of Abel.

Sick of Brother sick of Fellows
Blacks and Reds and Browns and Yellows
sick of each minority
pressing for autonomy
sick of white men ugly white men
arrogant and always right men
sick of sick men sick of sickness
Protestant- and Catholic-ness
sick of every lying bromide
Happy Birthday Merry Yuletide
freedom truth and brotherhood
Reader's Digest motherhood
pledge allegiance to the flag
"under God"—now what's the gag?

Sick of vicious ostentation
sick of humor's constipation
sick of sicknsss human sickness
human greed and human thickness.

Get my Brother off my back
White Red Yellow Brown and Black.
Perish Abel perish quick—
One of us is awful sick.

III

4:6 *Why are you angry, why are you downcast?*
4:7 *If you do well, will you not be accepted?*

If I do well? What do you mean by well?
I am the very symbol of respect.
You know me, J.B. Cain, the president
of Acme Company; presiding deacon
of my church. They say I *am* the church,
that no one moves a chair or spends a dime
belonging to the church without my knowledge
and my consent.

                    Or let me introduce
myself, Professor Cain. What can I say
but what is said: noted authority;
writer of books and brilliant articles;
dynamic lecturer, admired of students,
the envy of his colleagues. A modest man,
I live for learning and its meager fruits.
The adulation I but tolerate.
My one profession is the field of knowledge:
I spurn, for this career, all lesser goods.

If I do well? What do you mean by well?

I am a student here, one of the best.
Jonathan Cain the Third. I chose this school
(as did my father, Jonathan the Second
as did his father, Jonathan the First)
and was accepted here because I have
the proper gifts, the proper attributes.
Not only am I here, but I belong
(it is enough to say that I belong).
The contours of success are everywhere
apparent in my person and my station.
I am the son of parents who are right;
I am the product of the proper schools;
I am myself the rightest of the right.

If I do well? What do you mean by well?

Meet Luther Cain, the bright young minister.
Servant of God. I love thy kingdom, Lord,
the house of thy abode. I give myself
to thee and to thy church. And no mean gift
it is. I am an honor graduate
of Christian University where I
was student council president and triple
letter man. (They called me "Triple-threat"
not in the mundane football sense, but as
a triple threat in studies, sports, and love.)
I come to thee and to thy service, Lord,
equipped in mind and heart—and in physique.
Together we will lead thy people, Lord.

Why do you say to me, "If you do well"?
I am a doctor, lawyer, engineer.
I am a businessman, Rotarian.
I earn an honest wage, I pay my bills.
I give to feed the poor. I hate what must
be hated. I support the decent causes.
I am a Mason, thirty-third degree,
Knight of Columbus, Synagogue and Temple.
I am a Man, firstborn of Adam, son
of God, king of the universe. A Man!

If I do well—my God, what do you want?

IV

4:7 *If you do well, will you not be accepted?*

Acceptance is it now? You toss that out
as if it were a simple thing: do well
and be accepted. *Ganz einfach! Voila!*

It does not work that way. To be accepted
or not to be accepted is the question;
and if to be accepted, on what terms,
whose terms, by whom, with whom, and to what end?

I know you, Chief. I know your ancient problem.
The word about your nature gets around.
I know your universalistic leanings;
I know that you are gracious, merciful,
in anger slow, in steadfast love abounding.
This is, at least reputedly, the word.
This is your widely rumored reputation.

I hope you will not mind a mild rebuff:
deity should be made of sterner stuff.

You offer me acceptance, *on your terms*.
You will accept me—if I come with Abel.
And this is what you mean by doing well:
hold my revolting brother by the hand.

Let me propose the terms. If you want me,
you cannot have my brother. Damn it, God,
you know how rudely Abel comes between
the two of us. He fouls our sweet communion
where two is company and three's a crowd.
It is for you, for us, I cut him off!
Besides, my way is difficult enough,
my passage rough enough, my risky crossing
fraught enough with hazards of my own.

The choice to be or not to be accepted
is mine to make, and I have made the choice.
Acceptance on your terms is unacceptable:
As far as I'm concerned, Abel is dead.

V

4:8   *Let us go out into the field.* Come, Abel,
how shall I kill you? Let me count the ways,
since violence is versatile and knows
not only savage acts of massacre
by human malice or indifference,
but subtler forms as well, aesthetic forms
which spare the sight and smell of death and yet
remove the victim. Homicide can be,
on any scale, grotesque or beautiful.
Human community can be destroyed
in crude brutality or, if one will,
if one but exercise intelligence,
in fashion cold and clean and rational.

4:8   *So Cain rose up against his brother Abel*
and killed him. Yahweh said to killer Cain,
Where is your brother Abel? Where is Abel!
I do not know. Am I my brother's keeper?

VI

4:10   *What have you done? The voice of Abel's blood
is crying to me from the ground.* "The voice
of Abel's blood, a thousand million voices
crying to me from the bloody ground!

"O Cain, my son, my son, who took the life
of Abel, son of mine. The voice of Abel,
the voice of Abel's blood, is crying to me
from the bloody ground, the blood-soaked ground.
O Absalom, my son, my son, who took
the life of Amnon, son of mine; the voice
of Amnon, Absalom, is crying to me
from the ground. O bleeding son of mine,
the son your brother (son of mine) despised;
my son rejected, smitten, and afflicted;
my son, my wounded son, my dying son,
subjected to the public ways of dying
and all the countless, private, hidden ways—
in battle, execution, inquisition;
in lethal oven or in lethal humor;
in lynching by the hand of brutal brother;
or brutal psychological exclusion;
and always wholesale murder by neglect.

"My son, my son! The voice of Abel's blood
is crying to me from the ground. O Christ,
O Jesus Christ, my son, my dying son!"

VII

4:11–12 *Now cursed from the ground are you . . . it shall*
no longer yield its strength . . . a fugitive
and wanderer upon the earth are you.

4:13 My punishment is more than I can bear.
You curse me from the ground, the earth, the land;
the lovely land, the land of habitation;
the land of tent and temple, house and home;
the land of sound and singing; land of meeting;
the land of school and market; land of loving;
the land of birth and death and living passion;
the land of seeing, speaking, hearing, touching.

You curse me from the ground, and earth becomes
a curse and all its fullness—father earth;
productive mother earth; familial earth;
sister of faith and hope; consoling brother
of anguish; patient aunt, indulgent, loving;
the uncle, bluff and crude and roughly hearty;
the frail grandparent, shrunken and unknowing,
but holding on to life and holding on;
the winsome cousin, gaily violating
the old taboos, and scorning inhibitions;
and tender lover, spouse, the close companion.

VIII

You curse me from the ground—you curse my life!
The lovely land becomes the loveless land;
relationships which ought to give support
are sour, insubstantial, charged with doubt;
the earth, the bloody earth, is unresponsive;
and I—I am a bitter fugitive,
a restless wanderer upon the earth,
cut off from Abel *and from you!*

From you,
you stubborn God! I can't lay hold of you!
From your face I am hidden. Where are you?

Take back your bloody earth, your alien earth,
your loveless, lonely, godforsaken land.
This life, this bleak reality, is more
than anyone can bear. So come sweet death!

IX

4:15   Then Yahweh put a mark on Cain, a mark
on everyone, lest we forget that we
are not our own but God's, made in God's image.
So fugitives we are, God's fugitives;
and wanderers we are, God's wanderers;
until the day we learn to live as keepers,
when restlessness will be resolved in rest,
and lovelessness in love, and all estrangement
will be at last redeemed in death.

X

Whose death?

Whose son?

Whose brother?

Come sweet death!

part 12345

THE FLOOD

from Genesis 6—9

6:5 Yahweh saw that [human] wickedness was great in the earth, and that every imagination of the thoughts of [their] heart was only evil
6:6 continually. And Yahweh was sorry [for having] made "man" on the
6:7 earth, and was profoundly grieved. So Yahweh said, "I will blot out [all that] I have created from the face of the ground, [humankind] and beast and creeping things and birds of the air, for I am sorry that I have made them."

6:8–9 But Noah found favor in Yahweh's eyes. . . . Noah was a righteous man, blameless in his generation; Noah walked with God.

6:13—7:4 And God said to Noah, . . . "Make yourself an ark. . . . I will send rain upon the earth forty days and forty nights; and every living thing that I have made I will blot out from the face of the ground."

7:12, 21 And rain fell upon the earth forty days and forty nights. And all flesh died. . . .

8:13, 20 [When] the waters were dried from off the earth . . . Noah built an
8:21 altar to Yahweh. . . . And when Yahweh smelled the pleasing odor,
8:22 Yahweh said, . . . "While the earth remains, seedtime and harvest, cold and heat, summer and winter, day and night, shall not cease."

9:20–21 [Noah] planted a vineyard; and he drank of the wine, and became drunk, and lay uncovered in his tent. . . .

I

Genesis 6:5 And Yahweh saw the depth of human evil
upon the earth, that all the images
of mind and heart were constantly perverted.
6:6 And Yahweh looked in anguish at creation,
the creatures God had set alive and loved,
the splendid earth, the now-corrupted earth,
perverse, pernicious earth Yahweh had made;
and Yahweh was distressed and desolate.

remiah 8:18–20 "My grief is past all healing, and my heart
is sick within me. Hear the cry that rises
throughout the length and breadth of this creation:
'The harvest now is past, the summer ended,
and still we are not saved!' This wretched sickness,
this deep affliction, waits in vain for healing.
Hear now the crying, sense the brutal hatreds,
assay the stench, the rotting human stench,
and estimate the epidemic anguish.

the flood

Jeremiah 8:21 ff.   "For all the wounds of earth, *my* heart is wounded.
I mourn. Dismay has taken hold on me.
Is there no balm in Gilead? Or Rome?
No healing in Geneva? Is there then
no therapy in Paris or Beijing;
in Washington or London or Berlin?
Is there no antidote in Bogotá,
Johannesburg, Calcutta or in Seoul,
Jerusalem or Cairo or Beirut,
in Moscow or Manila or Madrid;
Belfast, Hong Kong, Tokyo, El Salvador?
Is there no balm in Gilead? Where, now,
physicians to attend this giant patient,
this earth, this sick creation, moribund,
but charging like the stricken, bleeding bull
to violent death? Is there no balm, no wisdom
compounded with compassion, and no love
sufficient for this mortal, earthly illness?"

II

Job 1:6 f. "I hear the Adversary coming now.
A busy and ambitious Son of God,
the quintessential gross male chauvinist."

"Ah, there you are, Eternal Majesty!
Dear Lord, kind Lord, and gracious Lord, I pray,
grant me a word with you, just for today."

"Whence have you come?" (as if I do not know).

"From going to and fro upon the earth,
from walking up and down the whole creation—
and may it please the King and Lord of all."

"What do you think?" (as if I do not know,
you thorny, suave, frustrated deity;
now here it comes, the charge that everything
awry in human history results,
of course, from my naive mismanagement).

"It is, O Lord, with infinite compassion
(in keeping with Our nature) that I roam
this sad creation. May I speak, O Lord,
in perfect candor (as befits Our station)?
Your great mistake in this abortive act,
this (be it said) exquisite formulation,
this enterprise so wondrously conceived
and executed (yes, indeed!): Your error
(and I speak with justified annoyance,
albeit with respect) is one of judgment.

"Earth is a mess (to call a spade a spade),
a godforsaken, catastrophic mess.
Precisely so, a godforsaken mess,
forsaken by the very God who made it.
Now hold your fire, let me finish—Sir.
I know, all of us know, about your Word,
your efficacious Word, the Word with power;
your Word in history, interpreting
(and possibly affecting or effecting)
particular events. All of us know.

"Your repertoire, of course, is out of balance;
you favor Palestinian events
and specialize in wonders wrought on water.
Look at your classic acts—the bringing up
of sickly little Israel from Egypt;
the founding of Davidic monarchy;
the bitter act of cataclysmic judgment
against your chosen people, contradicting
your own avowed intent; the re-creation
of Israel, a pale and sterile image
of what had been before. And then at last
(you have macabre tastes) your masterpiece,
the pièce de résistance, the mighty act
par excellence—a bloody crucifixion."

III

"A godforsaken, catastrophic mess!
Oh, you were there all right, it isn't that.

"All of us know (this is too obvious)
your tendency to hover, shall we say,
to brood upon earth's insolent estrangement.
But witness how you 'reign' in history.
It is, of course, your show; you give it meaning;
the whole vast operation feeds itself
upon your life and love, and is sustained
entirely by your will. Well, are you King
or slave? Assert yourself—or let it go!

"Your bourgeois notions of democracy
have now become the laughingstock of heaven.
You want to be *elected* God, you want
to reign by universal acclamation.
You entertain the ancient, feudal dream
of loving subjects in a loving kingdom
presided over by a loving ruler.

"They even talk about you in the heavenly host,
good-naturedly, of course, among themselves.
Some now refer to earth as Yahweh's folly.
I hear a few of them developing
the theme of Yahweh's yo-yo: 'You remember
the yo-yo Yahweh dotes upon . . . the job
complete with continents and mighty seas . . .
with tides and private, yellow satellite . . .
and creatures on its surface, little folk
who strut about, and play at being God. . . .
That yo-yo is defiant, mutinous,
and spinning on its own—or that is what
the crazy little creatures think and want . . .
and what does Yahweh do but brood and sulk,
and sit there grim and wounded, grieved and weeping.'

"Well, by the holy Word of God, how patient
are you supposed to be, how long in anguish?
You ape too much the weaker human virtues—
forgiveness, patience, love, and sweet compassion.
All these are female virtues, female fodder
in church and in the League of Women Voters.
Come, be a Man, for God's sake, be a Man.
Assume command! And act! Destroy the earth!"

IV

"Or, if to act in full annihilation
offends your godly love of rebel earth,
we'll simply for the moment dream a dream,
project a dream of total inundation
by which you start the earth again.

Genesis 6:8–9   "There's Noah.
Always there is the good and blameless Noah,
the gentle Noah, upright, righteous Noah
(whose name is also Job or Albert Schweitzer;
Mother and Saint Teresa, or Bonhoeffer;
or Daniel, Unamuno, short St. John;
or any of the thousands of the 'good').

"There's Noah over there, the peerless Noah,
the clean and honest Noah—noble Noah.
Wipe out the rest. Spare Noah, nifty Noah.
          Let God make another start,
              drawing from the pure in heart.
          God, become a remnant-maker:
              save the giver, drown the taker,
              drown the hater, spare the good,
              thus producing brotherhood.
          Suffering Lord and gentle Schemer,
              here's the dream—you be the Dreamer."

V

"A dream of yours, of course, is more than dream.
It always *is,* and in its dreadful *isness*
it teeters on the brink of history
or hangs, suspended by the merest thread,
above existence, threatening to fall
from dream to Word, from myth to dire fulfillment.
In *any* time of dreaming of this dream,
the dream *could* turn to stark reality.

"This dream of flood, by rain or radiation,
this dream of yours of lethal inundation—
this is a proper dream, *a proper act*
appropriate to the Maker and Sustainer
of life and earth and elemental nature,
as well as to secessionist creation.

"You and your silly notions of election!
The votes are being counted and the fact is
you haven't got a prayer. You're way behind
the leaders—Pentagons, Transnationals,
Trilateral Commissions, the elite
of humankind who *really* rule the earth.
You're even running second to some *Things:*
to Ships and Shoes and Sealing Wax and Cabbages;
to Institutions—Church and Bank and Bed.

"Now be a Man; for God's sake, be a Man.
Become a manly God and cut the thread.
Let fall the dream and bring for once and all
your anguish *and creation* to an end.

"And now, forgive me, Lord, if I have spoken
a word amiss. I speak, you know, in love."

VI

"Well, thank you, gentle Adversary. There,
the wind subsides, the mighty blow is gone
and I am God again—not 'man' nor male."

6:7   *I will blot out all of humanity*
        from off the earth . . . for I regret creation.

"Did I dream this; and shall I dream it now?
Is there then nothing for it but to drown it,
to snuff it out, extinguish it, erase it—
this heedless, insubordinate creation,
this sick, estranged, rebellious, bleeding earth;
this life, this love, this long intoxication,
this cherished, fabulous, unique existence?

           "Shall I now begin to shout,
           Blow that stinking candle out!
           Drifting, derelict domain—
           bury it in lethal rain!

7:4   "Forty days and forty nights
7:17 ff.   bury depths and bury heights,
           inundate the whole creation,
           every country every nation.
           Blot out everything with breath—
           perish life . . . and come sweet death.

"Wipe out the rest! Spare Noah, nifty Noah!"

VII

"And so, the dream, and I Yahweh, the dreamer.
Of course I ought to know (of course I know):
a self-perpetuating righteousness
exists in no one, let alone the race.
The dream goes wrong. What comes of all this rain,
this baptism, this death and resurrection?
What comes of this remarkable prescription
'Let God effect from righteousness (named Noah)
a new beginning: spark the ancient ruins
with nobleness and truth!' What comes of this?

9:20–25   "The gentle Noah soon is alcoholic,
and nakedness again becomes a problem.
8:21   The pleasing odor of the purged creation
begins again to reek of new pollution;
and we, the purged and Purger, folk and God,
are once again estranged. A sordid ending.
A somber, sorry, sordid new beginning."

60

VIII

"So let the dream of flood remain a dream.
I grieve in truth; but to assert control
I cannot go beyond my Word—the soft,
persistent Word, the Word that I have spoken
from time to time to some who know I speak
and some who do not know, but hear and speak
the Word again, unlabeled; paint the Word
or dance the Word or act the Word unmarked
and unidentified, but still the Word;
the Word made flesh, the Word by incarnation,
the Word that always *is,* however much
they try to say 'it was' or 'it shall be'!
Beyond the Word I cannot, will not, go."

IX

8:22 "While there is earth, while earth remains, these things
shall be: seedtime and harvest, cold and heat,
summer and winter, day and night—these things
shall be.

                      "And people, too—to feed the earth
and harvest it; to know and sense and savor,
to glory in and vehemently protest
the range and variation of the earth;
to make of it an idol or a demon;
to worship it or curse it; feel at one
with it, at home in it; or halting, stumbling
across its eyeless, unresponsive face
remain, as long as life remains, an alien
upon the earth, withdrawn, embittered, lonely.
As long as earth remains, these things shall be."

X

"But *I* shall be, my *Word* shall be, forever.
And what no lethal rain can bring about,
no righteousness effect, my Word shall do—
the Word that always is, the Word made flesh,
the Word of God Incarnate. . . . Come sweet death!"

12345

part

THE TOWER

from Genesis 11

1–2   Now the whole earth had one language and few words. And as [people] migrated in the east, they found a plain in the land of Shinar and settled there.

3   And they said to one another, "Come, let us make bricks, and burn them thoroughly." And they had brick for stone, and bitumen for mortar.

4   Then they said, "Come, let us build ourselves a city, and a tower with its top in the heavens, and let us make a name for ourselves, lest we be scattered abroad upon the face of the whole earth."

5
6   And Yahweh came down to see the city and the tower, which the [human family] had built. And Yahweh said, "Behold, they are one people, and they have all one language; and this is only the beginning of what they will do; and nothing that they propose to do will now be
7   impossible for them. Come, let us go down, and there confuse their language, that they may not understand one another's speech."

8
9   So Yahweh scattered them abroad from there over the face of all the earth, and they left off building the city. Therefore its name was called Babel, because there Yahweh scattered them abroad over the face of all the earth.

I

At this time all the earth was of one speech
and simple words. A treeless Eden.
A simple, single speech.
Contrast the present
babel.

II

They found a fertile valley in Shinar
and settled there. Shinar, is it?
or Shaker Heights or Shechem;
Sheboygan, Shanghai
Shiloh.

They talked among themselves of making brick.
"Come, burn the brick—it will endure—
and build the stalwart city
for us, ourselves.
For us.

"And let us make a tower for ourselves,
its head above all heights. And we
will scale the dizzying heights
ourselves, for us.
For us.

"We have at hand the stuff to join the brick.
So build it brick by burning brick,
a brick upon a brick.
The ruddy brick.
The Brick . . .

"All glory be to thee, O ruddy Brick,
almighty Brick that we have made,
O burned and burnished Brick,
our refuge and
our strength.

"This Brick, this mighty fortress, is our God,
a bulwark never, never failing;
our shelter from the flood
of mortal ills
prevailing.

"Ah blessed Brick that builds the steadfast city.
Ah wondrous tower, head in heaven.
On these we proudly stamp
our name—Produced
by Man.

"Security, the power to resist
dispersion—Made by Man: the means
of order and control
of destiny.
Amen."

III

Produced by Man—the rape of scores of cities
across the face of human history.
The ghastly inquisitions—Built by Man.
The ghettos, Jesus Christ, the bloody ghettos
Produced by Man; the rotten, stinking ghettos
in classic form a "Christian" institution
ordained, perpetuated, in the name
of Christ—O fraudulent appropriation!
The *barrios, favelas,* slums—all strewn
in hideous variety of form
across the loveless texture of the earth.

It is an ugly wonder that this Man,
created in the image of Creator
to be himself creator, turns his hand
with vast creative passion, tirelessly,
to works of death. An ugly wonder, this.

The function of Creator is inverted:
no longer is it order out of chaos,
and light called forth from darkness, life from death;
but chaos out of order, dark from light,
and death from life. An ugly, morbid wonder.
One hears the timeless cry, demonic shout,
from breathing, feeling, living godlike beings,
from throats alive and lusty—"Long live Death!"

A city and a tower and a name
produced by Man, destroyed by Man
in ceaseless, senseless cycle.
The pride of Man
is death.

IV

Yahweh came down, who never sleeps or slumbers.
God walks the garden; loves the brothers;
acts, in flood, in judgment;
and knows the tower
is death.

Yahweh came down. God comes. The life of God—
participating, anguished life—
impinges on existence
(invoked or not)
in love.

All silently and uninvoked God comes
to view the vast, pretentious city
and monumental tower
to human pride,
to pride!

God hears one calling to another, saying,

Luke 2:10–11 "Be not afraid; we have good news of joy,
great joy, to all of us. For unto us
is born this day a city and a tower.

Isaiah 9:6 The government shall be within the city
and we will make ourselves a name for us—
Wonderful Counselor, Almighty God
and Everlasting Father, Prince of Peace!

Luke 2:12 "And this shall be a sign for us—the tower,
the monumental tower touching heaven."

Luke 2:13–14 And suddenly there is the multitude
of earthly hosts all praising Man and saying,
"Now glory be to Man above the highest,
and in the city peace forevermore."

V

Genesis 2:7   "But it is I who breathe into your nostrils
the breath of life. Your breath is mine to give
or take away. I teach you how to walk,
not once upon a distant time, but now.
The step you take today you take with me.
You live and move and have your very being
in me, in my existence, in my life.
I always am, I AM, however much
you try to say I was—or never was.

Isaiah 29:16   "You turn things upside down! Will you regard
the potter as the clay? And is it right
for something made to say against the Maker,
'You made me not,' or something formed to say
to One who is the Former and Sustainer
of everything, 'You have no understanding'?

"Now see the wretched sum of it, this madness,
this monstrous folly of appropriation,
this mortal seizure of immortal power.
Your city and your tower become your tomb
when in your prideful dreaming I am dreamed
out of existence; when you put your trust,
your ultimate security, in that
which you have fashioned with your hands and mind."

74

VI

"Your name is Adam, falling from the tree,
the tower of your pride and independence,
in sight of lusty Eve. The tower builder.

"Or Cain, who from the height of Abel's murder
slips off into an anguished life of falling,
in conscious, deadly, swift descent to death
upon the lusting earth, the bloody earth,
from whence your brother's blood forever calls.
The tower builder, Cain.

                    "Or noble Noah,
the righteous Noah: from the mighty heights
above the flood, descending to the earth
and sinking in the mire, the lusting mire.
Noah, tower builder.

"Tower, Tower!"

Isaiah 2:12–17   "I have a day against all that is proud,
against all that is lifted up and high;
against all lofty things in nature which
become objects of human praise and worship—
        cedars of Lebanon
        oaks of Bashan
        all the high mountains
        and all lofty hills.
I have a day against all human pride,
against the posturing symbols of that pride—
        against the high towers
        and fortified walls
        against all the ships
        and magnificent craft!
And human haughtiness will be subdued
and human pride brought low. And I alone
will be exalted in that awful day."

VII

Yahweh

Exodus 3:14   "I AM" came down.
God comes. The life of God,
participating, anguished life,
impinges absolutely on our life.

The day
the awful day
is every day because
we cannot live by Things alone
but by the Word of judgment and redemption.

"Come then
let us go down
confusing there their speech
so that they cannot understand
the language of the city and the tower."

VIII

So you can take it, God, and keep it, God,
this thwarted life, this frustrated existence.
A something quite describable is missing:
we do not really speak to one another;
we do not really see and read each other.
A something sweet and soft and warm, responding
in words, in speech, in plain communication
is missing, wanting, absent—or illusive:
always, O God, so damnably illusive—
a something that is something like a Word . . .

This punishment is more than we can bear.
You render one an alien from the other.
North has no Word for South, nor South for North.
Intelligible speech begins—and then
abruptly ends in empty, tortured words.
We talk across the wide proliferation
of human boundaries, uneasy borders,
from home and church and school and neighborhood
to Salinger and Sartre, Brecht and Albee.
We bellow in our rage, "Why is it, then,
so goddam hard to talk, to speak a word?"
We shout our syllables frenetically
as if a violent delivery
were substitute for simple understanding.
In all of this bewilderment of words
you make us fugitives and wanderers
among ourselves and even in ourselves.

This punishment is more than we can bear.

IX

Hosea 11:9   "I bear it too, I who am God, not 'man,'
the Holy One among you, in your midst.
I hear the cry from out the length and breadth
of this creation, sensing brutal hatreds
unmediated by communication.
I measure the immeasurable anguish
of Wordless words in endless mutual flow,
a frantic, empty, incoherent traffic.
But I am God, not 'man,' the Holy One
among you, in your midst. I will not come,
I will not visit you, in simple wrath.
In judgment there will always be redemption.

"I have a day against the high and lofty,
a day of execution, on a cross;
an awful day—a height against all heights:
a single, lonely, sickening, dizzying height
to which a Man has climbed, the Son of Man.
This too, like any height, betokens pride,
but not of earth: this is the pride of God.
Here too the pride of height is death; but now
this pinnacle of pride becomes unique,
for in descent again to lusty earth,
to bleeding earth, life is restored again
to Man and 'man,' the earth is soothed and healed,
the mire itself redeemed and life renewed."

X

Come Lord
Babel is better.
The Word of God is heard
in shattered pride; and from your fullness
we will all receive . . . grace upon grace.

So come
O come sweet death
O come Incarnate Word
O come, O come Immanuel
and ransom captive, Wordless Israel.

12345

part

THE LAND

from Genesis 12 and 15

1 Now Yahweh said to Abram, "Go from your country and your
   kindred and your father's house to the land that I will show you.
2 And I will make of you a great nation, and I will bless you, and make
3 your name great, so that you will be a blessing. I will bless those who
   bless you, and [those] who curse you I will curse; and in you all the
4 families of the earth will be blessed." So Abram went, as Yahweh had
   told him.

15:6 And he believed Yahweh, [who] reckoned it to him as righteous-
      ness.

I

OK, Yahweh. Let's recapitulate.
Creation we can take, after a fashion—
the proposition that the cup of life,

Psalm 23:5 not, incidentally, always overflowing,
is given to us by Another: You;
Yahweh; Creator; Ground of Being; God;
the Source, the unknown Source; the unknown Giver.
You thought that we would know you from the gift,
that we would see you in the cup?
My Friend, it's hard enough to see ourselves!

Our grasp of the cup is uneasy, unsteady:
the handle is awkward, the contents too heady.
We juggle the cup holding falcon and dove,
with a fist of oppression in a white nylon glove.

II

OK, Yahweh. Let's recapitulate.
You gave the cup—not quite without a word,
but nothing more. An unobtrusive word,
a quiet word, sometimes a silent word.
And, we confess we don't know how to drink.
We cannot take this stuff you give.

Look back

Jeremiah 8:22, 11   across our years. There *is* no balm, no peace.
There is no common speech or language heard,

Psalm 19:3, 4   no voice, cohesive line, throughout the earth.
Our drunkenness unleashes flood upon
destructive flood on all of us. We drink
the cup and, stinko, make of all our sweet
and perilous encounters only Babel.

III

OK, Yahweh. Let's recapitulate.
In certain areas we've achieved finesse,
sophistication past imagination.
But God!—what most we need, we haven't got.
      We land people on the moon;
      our computers are a boon;
      we transform the ugly faces
      of our cities' vilest places.
      We've got ready to release
      what it takes to make wars cease—
          What ain't we got?
          We ain't got peace.
      We've got skill to sight the blind,
      ways to heal the fractured mind
      (while we covet neighbor's house
      and we sleep with neighbor's spouse).
      We've got God-in-heaven-above
      and the voice of turtledove—
          What ain't we got?
          We ain't got love.

IV

OK. So much for recapitulation.
So here we are, a new church generation,
new-minted in the new theology
(whatever that may be); fresh-coined, bold
in new experimental liturgy,
aware of all the brave new forms designed
to make the gospel come alive again.

(And parenthetically one wants to add:
whatever be the verdict of the doctors
on whether God is dead, or mutilated;
or maybe somehow sick—this allegation
of critical divine pathology—
whatever be the fact, while we inquired,
the Holy Spirit seemingly expired.)

Let us be truthful, God, since we affirm
no secrets hide from you; let us be frank.
We're scared. We're playing with a deck that's stacked.
The odds seem hopelessly against us now.
In faith we're called to take this whole sick world
as adversary, subject of our conquest.
And we go forth to battle, armed to teeth
with puny theological peashooters,
supported by a Word from you, itself
so unobtrusive as to warrant doubt.
We're scared. We're frightened at the *sound* of you!
We think the trumpet-voice, blasting our ears,
or silence, utter silence, would be better.

Isaiah 6:8   "Whom shall I send, and who will go for us?"
The question rings about as strong and true
as gramophone recordings of Caruso;
and our response, "Well, here we are, send us,"
is equally distorted, unconvincing.
We hear ourselves, unreal and automated,
our voices thin, devoid of resonance,
and wonder at this strange exchange,
this dreamlike insubstantial confrontation
between the called and Caller, both of whom
seem frail at best. Or worse, we play a game,
we stage a farce of mutual deception.

V

Isaiah's temple vision better suits
an age of quieter piety than ours.
Our temples are too busy doing the work
of temples; much too noisy in the task
of making temple sounds. Our temples temple.
From morning until night, frenetically,
they go about the busy work of templing.
We haven't anything against Isaiah.
It's only that we've got a *thing* with temples.

And there's another reason why we can't
authentically appropriate the vision:
our minds are much too busy being minds,
and much too noisy making thinking sounds.
From morning until night, frenetically,
we celebrate the work of cerebration.
We do not want to listen and respond.
We want to take command. We want to work,
manipulate, and cerebrate the Word.
In any case, the *hearing* of the Word
comes hard for us. The time, at least, is wrong.
In any case, Isaiah's vision suits
some other epoch better than our own,
some other age, some other generation.

VI

OK, Yahweh. Consider Abraham,
that legendary ancestor whose life
is told in ancient Israel in terms
appropriate to what that chosen people
then deemed their chosenness to mean and be.
The story of old Abraham was shaped
by Israel's corporate sense of entity
imposed upon a single man. The call
of Abraham is more than personal.
In Israel's faith, this is the Call *in essence.*

Genesis 12 ff.
The lie he told is everyone's deceit,
his greed, his lust, his self-concern are ours;
his crass unfaith, committed as it were
in the same breath with fervent affirmation,
is our unfaith. And his redemption, frail
and frangible, repeatedly in doubt,
assaulted vehemently by acts of pride,
is ours. The "patriarch" is everyone.

We're clear on this, Yahweh, and you must be.
I thought it well for you to know that we
all understand the nature of the text.

VII

OK. This is the essence of the call.

Genesis 12:1 The *language* of the call? "Go from your country,
and from your kindred and your parents' house.
Go to the land that I will show you!"

Great!
If we can read you straight and take the words
at superficial value—it's a breeze,
a cinch. No sweat. Who wants to live at home?
Who wants to live it all in Austinburg,
in Walton, Marion, or Cheverly?
Who wants to live and die in Lexington,
or Brooklyn, Pittsburgh, Closter, Menlo Park?
Who here aspires to go back home again?
Who wants to be a prophet without honor?

We are, Yahweh, the go-go generation,
and distant fields, in any case, are greener.

(But parenthetically you'll let me say:
if you expect to move us any distance,
you'll see that transportation is provided.
The move that Abram made to climes more sunny
was fine for Abraham: he married money.)

VIII

OK, Yahweh? I know, it's not OK.
It would be nice to take it so, so nice—
just break away and let you do the driving.
While we suspect the TV "church" of fraud,
they sometimes make it seem to us alluring;
and while we know it isn't all that simple,
sometimes the fundamentalists look good:
they have the straight, unvarnished Word of God.
The scheme is clear—no ambiguities.
Just leave, and God will take you to the land.
Accept the Lord and Savior, Jesus Christ
today, right now; and Peace, you're in the land.
Don't fornicate: you're in the land. Don't drink:
you're there. And read the Bible every day.
You'll have the overflowing cup of life,
the cup of grace, elixir, in the land.
And guard with care your own sweet soul's salvation—
you're in the land, the land is yours, the land
of milk and honey! Praise The Lord!

Oh yes.
Just one thing more. You'll want to *stay,* of course;
so keep it clean and personal. Don't foul
your antiseptic faith with politics
(unless, of course, it's firmly to the right);
don't mess in messy social enterprises.
You know the Word of God—it's in the Book—
give Caesar what is Caesar's. *Give God God's!*
And so, be fruitful in the promised land,
the land the Lord thy God hath given thee.

God, what a land! A lousy, lying land;
a dirty, stinking, bleeding, schizoid land!
Lord Jesus Christ, that's where we *are,* that's where
we've *been.* That's where we *started.* That's the land
from which you call us out, the very land
of country, kindred, land of father's house!

IX

Genesis 12:2–3

OK, Yahweh. We know it will not wash.
Where is the land to which you want to lead us,
endow us with a name, and make us great;
and bless the ones who bless us, curse our cursers;
and let *us* bless the families of the earth?
Where is this never-never land, Yahweh,
and where are you?—except in Jesus Christ.
We have to go and go and go and go,
perhaps not going anywhere, but going;
we have to go and go, and find the land,
and occupy the land—and *never* know,
and never *know* that we are in the land.

We lose the land, as ancient Israel learned,
when we possess the land, and claim the land,
and name the land, and call the land our own.

X

The land is come upon in doing the work,
redemptive work, of him who is the Word,
the unobtrusive Word, the quiet Word,
sometimes, it seems, the silent, hidden Word.

The land belongs to Christ, whose name is ours;
whose greatness we appropriate in love;
who, only, has the power of curse and blessing,
but by whose grace it can be given us
to bless the families of the earth.

                           Come, Christ,
in us!
                Come fresh again, sweet death, in us!
And in our dying from the ancient land,
bring us by our sweet death into the Land.

96